PAM'SDEMIC
A journey through my journal

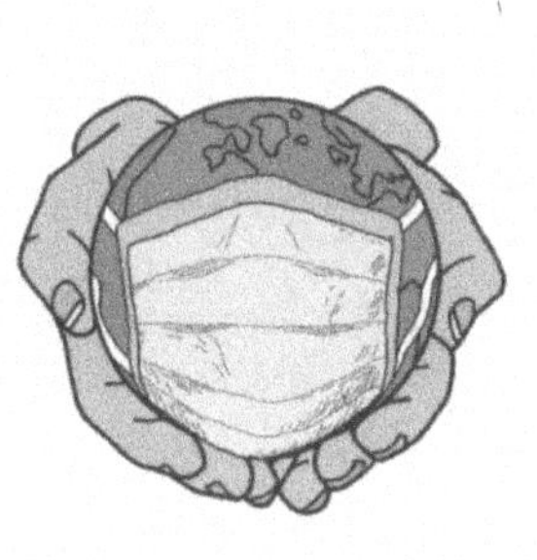

PAMELA GRIFFITHS

FORWARD

'Pam'sdemic a journey through my journal' is an account of what happened during the pandemic. This book is a general account of how the pandemic effected all of our lives.

Pamela Griffiths

A general review of Pamela's poetry

Publishing the work of Pamela Griffiths is one of the main reasons why I got involved in the world of poetry. I am a poet myself and I appreciate not just the upside of being a poet but also the very significant downside. Poetry is by nature, a lonely art. But it is very important art – not just to the poet, but to the poet's audience. Poetry is certainly an 'Outlet' for a person's feelings, but what good is an outlet without someone to read, understand and feel the emotions, passions and thoughts expressed in each poem?

Peter Quinn – Poet

London

DEDICATIONS

For my partner Sandy Hoffman
And all my family and friends

For all the people who have read my books and
encouraged me to carry on with my writing

For all the NHS staff and keyworkers.
For the people who volunteered and the fund raisers.
For all the people who helped us through the darker
days

Thank you

Pamela Griffiths

CONTENTS

ACKNOWLEDGMENTS

I WOULD LIKE TO THANK ALL MY FAMILY AND FRIENDS FOR
SUPPORTING ME THROUGHOUT MY WRITING YEARS.

THANK YOU TO GUEST AUTHOR JACK NEWMAN FOR CONTRIBUTING
ONE OF HIS POEMS INCLUDED AT THE END OF THIS BOOK

I WOULD ALSO LIKE TO THANK THE READERS WHO HAVE CONTINUED
TO SUPPORT ME BY PURCHASING MY BOOKS AND GIVING ME REVIEWS
AND FEEDBACK I THANK YOU ALL.

A BIG THANK YOU TO ALL THE NHS STAFF THAT HAVE HELPED US ALL
THROUGHOUT THE PANDEMIC.

THANK YOU TO ALL THE FRONTLINE WORKERS AND EVERYONE WHO
HAS HELPED US THROUGH THE DARK TIMES AND KEPT OUR SPIRITS UP.

PAMELA GRIFFITHS

1

A HAPPY NEW YEAR 2020

IT'S THE YEAR OF TWENTY TWENTY
WE'RE CELEBRATING IT IN STYLE
WE GO OUT FOR A MEAL AND SOCIALISE
DOING THINGS THAT MAKE US SMILE

WE HOPE THIS YEAR IS SPECIAL
LOOKING FORWARD OUR HOPES ARE HIGH
WE REJOICE AND LET THE NEW YEAR IN
SINGING AULD LANG SIGN WE CRY

LETTING GO OF THE YEAR THAT'S JUST GONE
WE HOPE THIS YEAR BRINGS GOOD LUCK
RESOLUTIONS ARE MADE FOR THE FUTURE
THIS NEW YEAR IS AN OPEN BOOK

AS WE START THIS YEAR WE ARE HOPEFUL
THIS YEAR WILL BE THE BEST
PLENTY OF TIME TO ENJOY THIS YEAR
A BLANK PAGE WE FILL IN THE REST

RING OUT THE OLD AND IN WITH THE NEW
THE START IS FULL OF GOOD CHEER
AS WE PUT THE OLD YEAR BEHIND US
WE WISH YOU A HAPPY NEW YEAR

WE DIDN'T KNOW BACK THEN AT ALL
HOW THINGS WOULD START TO UNFOLD
NOTHING COULD HAVE PREPARED US
FOR WHAT WE'RE ABOUT TO BE TOLD

NO ONE WOULD HAVE THOUGHT IT
WE DIDN'T HAVE A CLUE
A DEADLY VIRUS WAS ON ITS WAY
WE DIDN'T KNOW WHAT TO DO

SOMETHING BAD WAS ABOUT TO OCCUR
IT WAS COMING VERY FAST
BUT IT WAS JUST A VIRUS
SURELY IT WOULDN'T LAST

WE HADN'T SEEN ANYTHING LIKE IT
IT WAS DIFFERENT TO THE REST
WHAT WAS ABOUT TO FOLLOW
WAS A LIVING HELL AT ITS BEST

SO TWENTY TWENTY WAS DIFFERENT
NOT THE YEAR THAT WE HAD HOPED
AS THINGS PROGRESSED QUITE QUICKLY
IT'S A WONDER THAT ANYONE COPED

THIS HAPPY NEW YEAR WAS SHORT LIVED
SOON IT BECAME A YEAR FROM HELL
A YEAR WE WILL ALWAYS REMEMBER
WHAT A TALE FOR US ALL TO TELL

2

COVID 19
2020

IN THESE TERRIBLY DISTRRESSING TIMES
WE SHOULD THINK AND FEEL FOR OTHERS
WE ARE ALL IN THIS TOGETHER
WE'RE ALL SISTERS AND BROTHERS

WE SHOULDN'T APORTION BLAME
FOR WHAT WE CAN'T CONTROL
EVERYONE HAS THEIR USES
EVERYONE HAS A SOUL

THIS IS GLOBAL SHARING
NO ONE IS EXEMPT
EVERYONE NEEDS HELP NOW
WE'RE PAST TRYING TO PREVENT

LETS ALL PULL TOGETHER
WE HAVE TO FIGHT THIS THING
WHEN THE WORST IS OVER
WHO KNOWS WHAT THAT WILL BRING

THE VIRUS SPREADS ITS FURY
THROUGH THE DARKNESS WE SURVIVE
DOING WHAT WE CAN RIGHT NOW
TO TRY AND STAY ALIVE

NOTHING SEEMS TO STOP IT
AS WE ISOLATE FROM LIFE
THERE'S SO MUCH TO COPE WITH
IT STRIKES US LIKE A KNIFE

PEOPLE RALLY ROUND TO HELP
IT BRINGS OUT THE BEST IN SOME
WE TRY TO REMAIN POSITIVE
'TIL THIS VIRUS IS OVER AND DONE

NEVER IN OUR LIFETIME
HAVE WE HAD TO DEAL WITH THIS
WE HAVE NO PHYSICAL CONTACT
NO HUGS OR LOVING KISS

ALL THE FRONT LINE WORKERS
DO THE BEST THEY CAN
IF PEOPLE WOULD STAY IN AS TOLD
IT WOULD SAVE A TOTAL BAN

SO WE'RE ALL IN THIS TOGETHER
WE'RE GOING TO WIN THIS WAR
WE STAND UNITED AS A SHIELD
IN ISOLATION WE KNOW THE SCORE

TOMORROW IS ANOTHER DAY
AS EACH DAY ROLLS INTO ONE
WE HAVE TO STAY INSIDE AND SAFE
UNTIL THE VIRUS HAS GONE

WHEN ALL THIS IS OVER
WE CAN SEE EACH OTHER AGAIN
IT WILL MAKE US ALL REALISE
THINGS WILL NEVER BE THE SAME

LESSON'S WILL BE LEARNT FROM THIS
SO CHANGES MUST BE MADE
WE'RE PROUD OF ALL THE KEYWORKERS
AND PROUD OF THE LIVES THEY'VE SAVED

OUR NHS STAFF WERE FANTASTIC
THEY ALL WENT THAT EXTRA MILE
COMFORTING THE DYING AND SICK
WITH A CARING COMFORTING SMILE

ONE OR TWO THOUGHTLESS IDIOTS
TRIED TO SPOIL IT FOR THE REST
WE ALL CARED FOR EACH OTHER
UK PEOPLE ARE SIMPLY THE BEST

THROUGH POVERTY AND HARDSHIP
WE BATTLE ON THROUGH THE RAIN
ONE THING WE CAN BE CERTAIN OF
SOMEDAY WE'LL ALL MEET AGAIN

PARENTS ARE HOME SCHOOLING CHILDREN
SOME PEOPLE ARE WORKING FROM HOME
THANKS TO TODAY'S TECHNOLOGY
IT HELPS PEOPLE WHO LIVE ON THEIR OWN

WE KEEP IN TOUCH THROUGH FACETIME
SEND TEXTS AND SPEAK ON THE PHONE
WE CAN BE VIRTUALLY TOGETHER
WHICH HELPS PEOPLE LIVING ALONE

DRASTIC MEASURES ARE TAKEN
TO STOP THE VIRUS IN ITS TRACK
STAY SAFE SAVE LIVES STAY AT HOME
WE DON'T WANT THIS VIRUS BACK

SO WHEN THE LOCKDOWN IS OVER
OUR STIFF UPPER LIP CAN STAND DOWN
WE WILL ALL SEE EACH OTHER AGAIN
AND WE WILL OPEN UP OUR TOWN

3

A JOURNEY THROUGH MY JOURNAL

I WOKE UP THIS MORNING
EVERYTHING SEEMED SO WRONG
I BRUSHED MY HAIR AS USUAL
HECK IT HAS GROWN SO LONG

I DON'T EVEN KNOW WHAT DAY IT IS
EACH DAY ROLLS INTO ONE
EVERYTHING SEEMS SO VERY STRANGE
OH WHERE HAS MY LIFE GONE?

I AM SITTING HERE IN LIMBO
NOT KNOWING WHAT TO DO
EVERYONE ELSE IS SUFFERING
JUST LIKE ME AND YOU

GONE IS OUR NORMALLITY
AT FIRST OUR FEAR WAS UNFOUNDED
WE WERE TOLD TO STAY AT HOME
IN A FLASH WE WERE ALL GROUNDED

THEN ALL HELL BROKE LOOSE
THE VIRUS SPREAD LIKE WILDFIRE
SO NOW WE'RE ALL IN LOCKDOWN
SITTING IN OUR HOME ATTIRE

IT'S GETTING WORSE IT SEEMS
WE HAVE TO STAY INDOORS
WE'RE TRYING TO STAY SAFE AT HOME
PACING ALL THE FLOORS

FEELING LIKE CAGED ANIMALS
WE'RE NOT ALLOWED TO LEAVE
WE HAVE TO WASH OUR HANDS A LOT
AND SAFE DISTANCE I BELIEVE

FOR MONTHS WE ARE RESTRICTED
OUR HAIR GROWS LONG AND THICK
THIS STUPID AWFUL VIRUS
IS MAKING LOTS OF PEOPLE SICK

WE HAVE TO FOLLOW ORDERS
TO STAY SAFE AND FREE FROM HARM
IF WE ABIDE BY ALL THE RULES
THERE'S NO NEED FOR ALARM

AS NEW CASES REACH THEIR PEAK
THE DEATH RATE TAKES ITS TOLL
WE'VE FOLLOWED ALL THE GUIDELINES
WITH OUR HEART AND SOUL

GRADUALLY WE'RE ALLOWED TO LEAVE
THE CONFINES OF OUR HOMES
IT HELPS TO LIFT MANY SPIRITS
AND THE PEOPLE WHO LIVE ALONE

THIS IS DEFINITELY NOT OVER YET
WE STILL HAVE TO STAY STRONG
AS THINGS BEGIN TO UNFOLD AGAIN
THIS NEW NORM DOESN'T BELONG

WE WANT NORMALITY TO RETURN
BUT PERHAPS IT NEVER WILL
A VACCINE IS OUR ONLY HOPE
OR AN ANTI VIRUS PILL

AS I LOOK BACK THROUGH MY JOURNAL
IT INFORMS ME OF WHAT'S HAS GONE
TWENTY TWENTY WAS A YEAR FROM HELL
NOW IS THE TIME TO MOVE ON

15

4

A VIRTUAL HUG

I CAN'T VISIT OR SEE YOU IN PERSON
SO I'M SENDING A VIRTUAL HUG
IT'S HARD FOR EVERYONE AT THIS TIME
WHILE FIGHTING THIS VIRAL BUG

NOTHING CAN REPLACE A REAL HUG
BUT FOR NOW IT WILL HAVE TO WAIT
I CAN ONLY SEE YOU BRIEFLY
FROM THE END OF MY GARDEN GATE

A VIRTUAL HUG IS ALL I GET
ISOLATION TEARS ME APART
I WANT TO TOUCH AND HUG YOU
SEPARATION IS BREAKING MY HEART

BEHIND CLOSED DOORS I WEEP INSIDE
MY SOUL IS CRAVING NORMALLITY
I CAN'T DO ANYTHING TO CHANGE IT
I HAVE TO FACE THE NEW REALITY

I GAZE THROUGH AN OPEN WINDOW
THE WORLD HAS CHANGED SO MUCH
A SADNESS HAS COME OVER ME
AS I LONG TO HUG AND TOUCH

ONE DAY WE WILL ALL RETURN
TO NORMALLITY LIKE BEFORE
FOR THE MOMENT WE ARE PRISONERS
HIDING BEHIND A CLOSED DOOR

I LIVE IN HOPE IT'S ALL I'VE GOT
I LAUGH AND CRY WITH A SHRUG
I'M FEELING VERY GRATEFUL FOR
YOUR LOVE AND A VIRTUAL HUG

NEW SKILLS 2020

DURING THE LOCKDOWNS I KEPT BUSY
I SET MYSELF MANY NEW TASKS
LOTS OF PEOPLE ALL DID THE SAME
HELPING OTHERS AND MAKING MASKS

AT FIRST I STARTED BY PAINTING MY FENCE
THAT TOOK ME A LONG WHILE TO DO
WHEN I'D FINISHED THAT MAMMOTH TASK
I HAD TO FIND SOMETHING NEW

I ORDERED SOME FLAT PACK FURNITURE
I COMPLETED QUITE A FEW
THE UNITS LOOKED VERY NICE IN PLACE
NOW I NEED SOMETHING ELSE TO DO

I USED TO CROCHET MANY YEARS AGO
I DECIDED TO TRY IT ANEW
I'D FORGOTTEN HOW TO DO IT
SO THIS SKILL WAS LONG OVERDUE

I RETAUGHT MYSELF HOW TO CROCHET
I DID PROJECTS LIKE NEVER BEFORE
SOON I BECAME PROFICIENT AGAIN
AND I CROCHETED TOYS GALORE

LEARNING NEW SKILLS KEPT ME BUSY
I DIDN'T HAVE TIME TO DWELL
MY MIND WAS ALWAYS OCCUPIED
THROUGH THOSE LOCKDOWN DAYS OF HELL

6

NATURE

NATURE IS A WONDERFUL THING
IT WILL ALWAYS TRY TO SURVIVE
WHATEVER LIFE THROWS AT US
NATURE TRIES TO KEEP US ALIVE

WHILE WE WERE IN LOCKDOWN
IT HELPED OUR PLANET TO LIVE
THE AIR WAS SO MUCH CLEANER
NATURE HAS SO MUCH TO GIVE

THE VIRUS HAD STOPPED THE WORLD
BUT THE ANIMALS WERE FREE
THEY CARRIED ON REGARDLESS
NATURE WILL LET IT BE

WE ARE TO BLAME FOR DESTROYING
NATURE'S WONDERFUL THINGS
WE DESERVE TO HAVE RESTRICTIONS
NATURE HAS REASONS FOR WHAT IT BRINGS

WE GET LOTS OF ADVERSE WEATHER
WILDLIFE HAS A LOT OF STRESS
GLOBAL WARMING ISN'T HELPING US
BUT NATURE IS HERE TO IMPRESS

WE NEED TO SAVE OUR PLANET
WHILE THERE IS STILL TIME FOR CHANGE
NATURE CAN ONLY DO SO MUCH
THERE'S SO MUCH TO REARRANGE

AS I LOOK BACK

AS I LOOK BACK WITH SADNESS
AT LIFE BEFORE THIS BEGAN
I AM FINDING IT HARD TO REMEMBER
THIS EFFECTS EVERY WOMAN AND MAN

WITH THE EASING OF RESTRICTIONS
I AM FRIGHTENED OF THE RESULT
THERE ARE SO MANY PEOPLE OUT THERE
THAT IT MIGHT TURN INTO A CULT

AT THE END OF THE DAY IT WILL HAPPEN
THERE HAS TO BE A WAY OUT
NO ONE CAN EVER PREDICT
WHAT THIS VIRUS IS ALL ABOUT

ALTHOUGH I FEEL VERY VULNERABLE
I WILL HAVE TO FACE THE FACT
THAT WHATEVER HAPPENS NOW
WE MUST USE COMMON SENSE AND TACT

WE WILL HAVE TO LEARN TO LIVE WITH IT
THERE IS NOTHING MUCH WE CAN DO
I KNOW THAT I WILL DO WHAT I CAN
TO RESTART MY LIFE ANEW

YES I AM VERY FEARFUL NOW
I CAN'T RELAX AT ALL
ENGLAND HAS PUT ITS PRIDE FIRST
AND PRIDE COMES BEFORE A FALL

AS I LOOK BACK AT WHAT'S HAPPENED
I DON'T KNOW WHAT TO DO
LIFE WILL GO ON REGARDLESS
WHAT TO DO? WELL I HAVE'NT A CLUE

THINGS HAVE CHANGED FOREVER
SOME THINGS FOR THE BETTER I'M SURE
THE ONLY THING AS I LOOK BACK
IS WE REALLY DO NEED A CURE

PAM'SDEMIC

WE ARE IN THE MIDDLE OF A PANDEMIC
IT HAS SPREAD WORLDWIDE IT SEEMS
THE WORLD STOOD STILL FOR SOME TIME
SHATTERING EVERYONE'S DREAMS

I HAVE MY OWN PANDEMIC
I HAVE NAMED IT AFTER ME
THE VIRUS IS ALL AROUND US
ITS STILL THERE BUT I CAN'T SEE

IN MY PANDEMIC I HAVE NO CHOICE
I HAVE TO COMPLY WITH THE RULES
THE CHILDREN ARE GOING BACK AGAIN
SAFELY TO THEIR SCHOOLS

SHOPS ARE OPENING AND LETTING US IN
AS LONG AS WE OBEY THE SIGNS
WEARING FACE MASKS IN PUBLIC PLACES
SOME MASKS HAVE FUNNY DESIGNS

IN MY PANDEMIC I TRY TO STAY SAFE
WHILE OTHERS ARE FLOUTING THE LAW
FINES ARE GIVEN IF WE BREAK THE RULES
EVERYONE KNOWS THE SCORE

I AM LIVING IN MY OWN LITTLE WORLD
TRYING NOT TO STRESS TOO MUCH
I MISS MY FRIENDS AND FAMILY
AND I MISS BEING ABLE TO TOUCH

I KNOW I'M NOT THE ONLY ONE
WHO HAS TO LIVE WITH THIS PAIN
I'M IN MY OWN PANDEMIC
IN MY OWN LITTLE BUBBLE AGAIN

EVENTUALLY ALL THIS CHAOS WILL END
ITS TAKING SUCH A LONG TIME
SO UNTIL THEN I'LL WRITE SOME NOTES
IN THIS JOURNAL OF MINE

9

DEPRESSION

DURING THE LOCKDOWN I FIGHT THE
DEPRESSION
I TRY NOT TO DWELL ON THE COMING
RECESSION
I KEEP MYSELF BUSY TO USE MY FREE TIME
TRYING TO SMILE AS THOUGH EVERYTHINGS
FINE

INSIDE I FEEL THE DEEP DARKNESS RISE
I WAKE UP EACH MORNING WITH TEARS IN MY
EYES
I SET MYSELF TASKS TO GET THROUGH THE
DAY
WISHING THE VIRUS WOULD JUST GO AWAY

I'M FRIGHTENED FOR MYSELF AND OTHERS
I TOSS AND TURN UNDERNEATH THE COVERS
SLEEP WON'T COME AND I'M SO VERY TIRED
EACH DAY IS THE SAME NOT TO BE DESIRED

THERE SEEMS NO POINT IN GETTING DRESSED
LOUNGING CLOTHES SEEM TO BE THE BEST
NO ONE CAN SEE ME ANYWAY
SO HERE I AM ITS ANOTHER DAY

EVERY DAY BEGINS EXACTLY THE SAME
NO SIGN OF A BUS OR A TRAIN OR PLANE
HAS THE WORLD GONE MAD OR IS IT ME
IT IS WHAT IT IS WHAT WILL BE WILL BE

I'M IN A DARK PLACE I CANT GET OUT
I FEEL LIKE I COULD SCREAM AND SHOUT
THERE'S NOTHING I CAN DO OR SAY
THAT CAN MAKE THE DARKNESS GO AWAY

I TRY TO THINK POSSITIVE BUT ITS VERY HARD
I AM FEELING ON EDGE AND ON MY GUARD
I FEEL FEAR INSIDE IT WON'T GO AWAY
I FIND A SAFE PLACE THAT'S WHERE I'LL STAY

I'M HIDING MYSELF AWAY FROM IT ALL
NOT WANTING FRIENDS OR FAMILY TO CALL
ALL I WANT IS TO HIDE TODAY
WAKE ME UP WHEN ITS ALL GONE AWAY

10

FOUR O CLOCK IN THE MORNING

IT'S FOUR O CLOCK IN THE MORNING
I'M HAVING PROBLEMS GETTING TO SLEEP
MY MIND IS WORKING OVERTIME
STORING THINGS I DON'T WANT TO KEEP

STILL WIDE AWAKE WITH TORMENT
EVERYTHING IS SO STRANGE
NOTHING IS THE SAME ANYMORE
MY THOUGHTS I MUST REARRANGE

THE MORE I TRY TO SETTLE MYSELF
UPHEAVAL IS IN MY MIND
I TRY TO REMOVE THE NEGATIVE THOUGHT
THEY KEEP ON RETURNING I FIND

SO AS I LIE HERE WIDE AWAKE
TOSSING AND TURNING ALL NIGHT
I TRY TO SHRUG OFF THIS DEPRESSION
BEFORE THE MORNING LIGHT

I LISTENED TO THE BIRDS AWAKENING
THINKING THIS CANNOT BE RIGHT
HERE I AM AT FOUR IN THE MORNING
AND ITS STARTING TO GET LIGHT

I MAKE A MENTAL NOTE TO MYSELF
THIS REALLY HAS TO BE STOPPED
I CLOSE MY EYES LONGING FOR SLEEP
THEN INTO MY MIND THE THOUGHTS POPPED

HOPEFULLY THINGS WILL CALM DOWN SOON
SO I CAN SLEEP BEFORE FOUR IN THE
MORNING
ANOTHER NIGHT HAS DISAPEARED
I'M SHATTERED AND I CAN'T STOP YAWNING

27

SELF PITY

I WALLOW IN SELF PITY
IN THIS DARK AND DISMAL PLACE
I HAVE TRIED SO VERY HARD
TO PUT A SMILE BACK ON MY FACE

NO MATTER HOW I TRY
I STILL FEEL THE SAME
ITS NOW ANOTHER YEAR
REPEATING THE LAST YEAR AGAIN

NOTHING MUCH HAS CHANGED
WE'RE IN LOCKDOWN NUMBER THREE
WAITING FOR MY VACCINE JAB
HOWEVER LONG IT MAY BE

SO I'M WALLOWING IN SELF PITY
FEELING DOWN AND DEPRESSED
IS THERE NO END TO THIS?
THIS VIRUS DOES NOT REST

I TRY TO REGAIN MY CONFIDENCE
GET BACK MY SELF ESTEEM
BUT THIS VIRUS STILL LOOMS OVER US
LIKE AN EVIL KILLING MACHINE

AS THE DEATH RATE KEEPS ON RISING
MY SPIRIT DESCENDS SO LOW
I'M WAITING FOR THE TIME
WHEN THE VIRUS LETS US GO

I TRY NOT TO DWELL ON THE DOWNSIDE
SELF PITY WILL NOT HELP MY MOOD
I MUST TAKE EACH DAY AS IT COMES
TRYING HARD NOT TO BINGE ON FOOD

THERE IS LIGHT AT THE END OF THE TUNNEL
BUT ITS STILL A LONG WAY OFF YET
I MUST TRY TO STOP THE SELF PITY
BECAUSE CRYING JUST MAKES MY FACE WET

THE THINGS I TOOK FOR GRANTED

I MISS ALL THE THINGS I USED TO DO
IT WAS ALL SO NORMAL THEN
EVERYTHING HAS CHANGED SO MUCH
WILL IT EVER RETURN AND WHEN?

I TOOK EVERYTHING FOR GRANTED
I AM GRIEVING FOR THE PAST
I WANT TO RETURN TO HOW IT WAS
I DON'T WANT THIS TO LAST

NOTHING IS THE SAME ANYMORE
I CAN'T SEE MY GRANDKIDS NOW
I TOOK ALL THESE THINGS FOR GRANTED
I WANT TO GO BACK THERE SOMEHOW

I USED TO GO OUT AND CALL IN A CAFÉ
HAVE SOMETHING NICE TO EAT
I'D MEET UP WITH FRIENDS AND CHAT
PRECIOUS MOMENTS THAT I CAN'T BEAT

TAKEN FOR GRANTED WHEN ALL WAS WELL
I APPRECIATE EVERYTHING NOW
PEOPLE ARE RESTRICTED AND SAD
ALL I CAN SAY AT THE MOMENT IS WOW

RESTRICTIONS HAVE BEEN LIFTED
FOR SOME IT DIDN'T LAST LONG
THE VIRUS IS RETURNING AGAIN
THIS WHOLE THING SEEMS SO WRONG

13

IN TIMES LIKE THESE

IN TIMES LIKE THESE
WE HAVE TO THINK OF OTHERS
WE HAVE TO TAKE CARE OF
OUR SISTERS AND OUR BROTHERS

IN TIMES LIKE THESE
WE HAVE TO ALL PULL TOGETHER
WE NEED HELP TO SURVIVE THIS
BUT IT WON'T LAST FOREVER

LESSONS MUST BE LEARNED
WE HAVE ALL SINNED AT TIMES
ASKING FOR FORGIVENESS
WE MUST NOT IGNOR THE SIGNS

IF WE CAN WORK TOGETHER
WE CAN CHANGE THE NEGATIVE THINGS
IN TIMES LIKES THESE
WE WILL SEE WHAT TOMORROW BRINGS

WE ARE STUCK IN LIMBO
IN A VIRTUAL TIME FREEZE
STAY STRONG AND LOVING
IN TIMES LIKE THESE

WE WILL GET THERE IN THE END
IT WILL BE A LONG TIME YET
ITS IN TIMES LIKE THESE
WE WILL NEVER FORGET

THE ROAD MAY BE A LONG ONE
WE WANT IT ALL TO END
IT'S IN TIMES LIKE THESE
THAT WE REALLY NEED A FRIEND

INTO A SECOND LOCKDOWN

OH NO NOT AGAIN THIS IS AWFUL
INTO A SECOND LOCKDOWN NOW
APPARENTLY THIS IS NEEDED
TO CURB THE VIRUS SOMEHOW

THIS TIME THE SCHOOLS REMAIN OPEN
BUT BUSINESSES HAVE TO SHUT
SOME HAVE ONLY JUST OPENED
MANY STAFF HAVE TO TAKE A PAY CUT

SOME JOBS ARE LOST FOREVER
ITS HEART BREAKING FOR SO MANY
MANY STRUGGLE WITH THEIR MENTAL
HEALTH
TRYING TO SURVIVE WITHOUT A PENNY

IT WILL SOON BE CHRISTMAS
IT WON'T BE LIKE BEFORE
TRADITIONS WON'T BE THERE NOW
IF WE CAN'T GO OUT OF THE DOOR

NOTHING IS THE SAME THIS YEAR
ITS NEVER BEEN LIKE THIS BEFORE
WE CAN'T MEET UP WITH FAMILY
I CAN'T TAKE THIS ANYMORE

I POSTED MY CHRISTMAS CARDS EARLY
TO AVOID AN INEVITABLE RUSH
MY HEART JUST ISN'T IN IT NOW
TEARS FLOW FROM MY EYES WITH A GUSH

THERE IS TALK THAT WE MAY GET A VACCINE
I HOPE AND PRAY THIS IS SO
WE'RE INTO A SECOND LOCKDOWN
WE NEED THIS VIRUS TO GO

CHRISTMAS 2020

CHRISTMAS THIS YEAR WILL BE DIFFERENT
LOCKDOWN TWO FOR US WAS A BLOW
BUT WE REALLY NEED TO DISTANCE
OURSELVES
THE SHOPS WILL REOPEN I KNOW

NO CHRISTMAS CHEER OR SINGING
WE CAN'T CELEBRATE LIKE BEFORE
AND WHEN OUR CHRISTMAS IS OVER
THE VIRUS RETURNS ONCE MORE

EVEN STRICTER RESTRICTIONS
WILL HAVE TO BE PUT INTO PLACE
WHAT A DREADFUL YEAR IT'S BEEN
THIS WASN'T A HAPPY PLACE

WE HAVE TO PROTECT OUR BUSINESSES
OUR FAMILIES AND OUR SCHOOLS
THAT'S WHY WE MUST BE SENSIBLE
AND FOLLOW THE VERY STRICT RULES

THIS YEAR HAS BEEN A NIGHTMARE
WE'LL BE GLAD WHEN ITS GONE
TO PUT IT ALL BEHIND US NOW
SO THAT WE CAN CARRY ON

IT'S A YEAR THAT I'VE LOST FOREVER
I WON'T GET IT BACK AGAIN
ALL I HAVE ARE THE MEMORIES
AND THE VIRUS HAS A NEW STRAIN

LETS RING OUT THE OLD YEAR
AND LET THE NEW ONE IN
ITS TWENTY TWENTY ONE
A NEW YEAR IS ABOUT TO BEGIN

THE VACCINE

THERE IS TALK OF A VACCINE
THEY ARE TRYING TO RUSH IT THROUGH
IT SOUNDS PROMISING THEY TELL US
BUT WHAT COULD IT DO TO YOU?

I FOR ONE WILL HAVE IT
ANYTHING IS BETTER THAN THIS
JUST MAKE SURE ITS TESTED AND SAFE
THAT IS MY ONLY WISH

AFTER A YEAR LIKE THIS ONE
EVERYONE IS FEELING LOW
WE NEED SOMETHING TO LOOK FORWARD TO
THE VACCINE COULD MAKE IT SO

WHEN THE VACCINES ARE READY
I'LL BE FIRST IN THE QUEUE
I WANT TO HELP TO STOP COVID
IT'S THE LEAST THAT I CAN DO

THE NEWS ON THE VACCINE IS PROMISING
SO HOPE IS ALMOST IN SIGHT
BRING ON ALL THE VACCINES NOW
AND GIVE US A CHANCE TO FIGHT

THERE ISN'T MUCH LEFT OF OUR COUNTRY
WE MUST SALVAGE WHAT WE CAN
WE STICK OUT OUR ARMS TO FIGHT THIS
TO SAVE EVERY WOMAN AND MAN

TWENTY TWENTY A YEAR OF DISASTER
CAN BE WRITTEN OFF WHEN ITS DONE
SO BRING OUT ALL THE VACCINES PLEASE
BEFORE NEXT YEAR HAS BEGUN

TURN BACK TIME

I WISH I COULD TURN BACK TIME
TO WHAT I HAD BEFORE
THINGS WE TOOK FOR GRANTED
ARE NOT THE SAME ANYMORE

IF ONLY WE COULD HAVE FORESEEN
HOW THINGS WOULD DRASTICALLY CHANGE
WE WOULD HAVE MADE THE MOST OF LIFE
BUT NOW THAT'S OUT OF RANGE

IF I COULD REALLY TURN BACK TIME
AND KNOW WHAT I KNOW NOW
I WOULD HAVE DONE THINGS DIFFERENTLY
MADE THE MOST OF MY LIFE SOMEHOW

BUT THAT WON'T HAPPEN NOW
LIFE HAS CHANGED BEYOND COMPARE
IF ONLY I COULD TURN BACK TIME
TO GO BACK AND BE AWARE

ITS HARD WHEN I LOOK BACK
TO THE WAY IT WAS BEFORE
KNOWING HOW IT WAS FOR US
WE CAN'T HAVE THAT ANYMORE

IF I COULD TURN BACK TIME
I WOULD ALWAYS STAY IN TOUCH
PEOPLE ARE IMPORTANT TO ME
I HAVE MISSED THEM ALL SO MUCH

IT'S A SHAME THAT WON'T HAPPEN
TIME HAS BEEN AND GONE
BUT I KNOW WHAT'S NOW IMPORTANT
AS I LOOK FORWARD AND MOVE ON

ITS NOT OVER

UNFORTUNATELY THIS IS NOT OVER
WE STILL HAVE MUCH MORE TO ENDURE
IT COULD GO ON FOREVER
OR WE MIGHT JUST FIND A CURE

WHAT EVER HAPPENS FROM THIS POINT
IS NOW JUST SPECULATION
LIFE WILL KEEP ON GOING
AMIDST A MASS INOCULATION

ITS HIDING IN THE CORNERS
WAITING TO LATCH ON TO US
NOTHING HAS BEEN ABLE TO STOP IT
ITS WHAT THIS VIRUS DOES

SOMETIMES BECAUSE WE CAN'T SEE IT
WE FORGET ITS STILL THERE IN THE WINGS
THEN THE OUTBREAK GETS MUCH WORSE
IT AIN'T OVER 'TILL THE FAT LADY SINGS

SO CAREFULLY WE GET ON WITH LIFE
TRYING NOT TO FORGET IT'S THERE
ITS SCARY TO THINK IT IS WAITING
WE MUST BE AWARE AND TAKE CARE

I WANT AND NEED MY LIFE BACK

I WANT AND NEED MY LIFE BACK
AS MANY PEOPLE DO
I NEED TO SEE A FUTURE
TO MAKE MEMORIES ANEW

MY THOUGHTS HAVE CHANGED IMMENSLEY
I CAN'T TAKE THIS ANYMORE
I REALLY NEED MY LIFE BACK
TO THE WAY IT WAS BEFORE

EACH TIME THINGS SEEMED TO GET BETTER
WE HAD LETS DOWNS ALL THE WAY
I WANT AND NEED MY LIFE BACK
BUT THIS VIRUS IS HERE TO STAY

THE VACCINES HAVE HELPED US
IT'S A STEP FORWARD ITS TRUE
BUT THIS IS FAR FROM OVER
THERE ISN'T MUCH MORE WE CAN DO

PLEASE LET US HAVE OUR LIVES BACK
ALL THE THINGS WE USED TO DO
WE TOOK IT ALL FOR GRANTED
ONLY IN HINDSIGHT WE KNEW

I WANT AND NEED MY LIFE BACK
IT'S A BLUR AND ALL IN THE PAST
PLEASE LET US HAVE OUR FREEDOM BACK
THIS TIME WE MUST MAKE IT LAST

LOCKDOWN THREE

AFTER CHRISTMAS WE HAD LOCKDOWN THREE
THIS LOCKDOWN WAS A BAD ONE
EVERYONE WAS GROUNDED AGAIN
BUT THIS ONE WENT ON AND ON

WE WERE HOPING AFTER CHRISTMAS
THE NEW YEAR WOULD BE THE ONE
A YEAR TO HAVE OUR FREEDOM BACK
AND FOR THE VIRUS TO HAVE GONE

THE FIRST FEW MONTHS WERE AWFUL
THE WINTER MONTHS DRAGGED ON
THIS WAS WORSE THAN THOSE BEFORE
IT WAS HARSH FOR EVERYONE

WE THOUGHT THAT IT WOULD NEVER END
THIS TIME IT WAS DARK FOR ALL
OUR ONLY HOPE WAS TO GET A JAB
BUT WE WOULD HAVE TO WAIT FOR A CALL

AS THE MONTHS DRAGGED ON
I WAITED AND HOPED
I PUT ON LOTS OF WEIGHT
AND I BARELY COPED

LOCKDOWN THREE WAS HORRENDOUS
I DIDN'T WANT TO GO OUTSIDE
EVEN WHEN I'D HAD MY FIRST JAB
I JUST STAYED AT HOME AND CRIED

I HAD TO GET BACK ON TRACK
THIS WAS REALLY NOT LIKE ME
RESTRICTIONS WERE EASING SLOWLY
I VENTURED OUT GRADUALLY

THE SHOPS WERE ALL REOPENING
THE PUBS HAD OPENED OUTSIDE
WE COULD MEET UP WITH PEOPLE AGAIN
I KNEW THEN THAT I COULDN'T HIDE

I MUST GET OVER THIS AWFUL DREAD
BECAUSE MY SECOND JAB IS DUE
THERE'S A LIGHT AT THE END OF THE TUNNE
TO LOOK FORWARD IS WHAT I MUST DO

NOW HAVING HAD MY SECOND JAB
I FEEL MUCH SAFER NOW
WE'RE BACK ON TRACK TO NORMALITY
I KNOW WE'LL GET THERE SOMEHOW

THIS SUMMER SHOULD BE FANTASTIC
JUST LIKE IT USED TO BE
I HAVE TO REMAIN POSITIVE
IT'S THE START OF A FUTURE FOR ME

21

MOVING ON

WE'VE GOT A NEW HEALTH SECRETARY
THE OLD ONE GOT CAUGHT OUT
BREAKING RULES AND FILMED SOMEHOW
THERE'S A SNOOPY SPY ABOUT

A NEW HEALTH SECRETARY CAME
AND TOOK OVER TO REVEAL
RESTRICTIONS WILL BE LIFTED SOON
I DON'T KNOW HOW I FEEL

THE LIFTING OF RESTRICTIONS
IS A VERY RISKY THING
NO SAFE DISTANCING AND FACEMASKS
LET'S SEE WHAT THAT WILL BRING

I WANT MY FREEDOM BACK AGAIN
JUST LIKE EVERYONE ELSE DOES TOO
BUT I FEEL VERY FEARFUL
OF WHAT THIS MIGHT MEAN OR DO

IF WE DON'T TAKE THE CHANCE
WE WILL NEVER BE FREE AT ALL
COVID WILL ALWAYS BE WITH US NOW
SO WE HAVE TO MAKE THE CALL

I MYSELF STILL FEEL FEARFUL
I HAVE UNDERLYING CONDITIONS
FACEMASKS AND SAFE DISTANCING HELPED
TO PROTECT FROM THE VIRUS TRANSMISSIONS

I'VE HAD BOTH OF MY VACCINATIONS
IT WILL HELP TO GET ME THROUGH
I WILL HAVE TO TRUST IN FAITH
THAT'S ALL THAT I CAN DO

WE ALL HAVE TO LEARN TO LIVE WITH THIS
IT WILL NEVER GO AWAY
SO COMMON SENSE IS CALLED FOR
BECAUSE THIS BUG IS HERE TO STAY

BOOSTER JABS 2021

THEY'RE TESTING A BOOSTER VACCINE
IN CASE WE NEED IT SOON
IT'S BEING TESTED BY SOME VOLUNTEERS
IN THIS MONTH OF JUNE

WE DON'T KNOW IF WE'LL NEED IT
BUT IT HELPS TO HAVE ONE READY
AS WE EMERGE TO FREEDOM
WE WILL HAVE TO TAKE IT STEADY

WE MAY NEED YEARLY BOOSTERS
WE DON'T KNOW THAT FOR SURE
IF WE DO NEED BOOSTER JABS
WE WILL NEED A JAB ONCE MORE

HOPEFULLY WE WILL GET ONE
IF ITS NECESSARY TO SURVIVE
RIGHT NOW WE WILL DO ANYTHING
TO KEEP OURSELVES ALIVE

IT LOOKS LIKE THE VIRUS IS HERE TO STAY
PROTECTION IS OUR ONLY HOPE
BOOSTER JABS WILL HELP US THROUGH
SO THE HOSPITALS CAN STILL COPE

WE DON'T WANT ANY MORE LOCKDOWNS
THIS COULD GO ON FOREVER
IF BOOSTER JABS IS WHAT IT TAKES
WE CAN ALL GET THROUGH THIS TOGETHER

23

SPORT

SPORT IS NOW RETURNING
THE SPORTS WE ALL ONCE KNEW
ENGLAND CAN BE PROUD
DOING WELL IN WHAT WE DO

DESPITE ALL THE RESTRICTIONS
SPORT RETURNS TO ITS FORMER GLORY
CRICKET, TENNIS AND RUGBY
ARE ALL TELLING A NEW STORY

FOOTBALL'S COMING HOME AGAIN
IN LOTS OF DIFFERENT WAYS
CHANGING FOR THE BETTER
LIKE BACK IN THE OLD DAYS

WIMBLEDON SEEMS ALMOST NORMAL
IT'S GOOD TO SEE IT RETURN
LOTS OF NEW YOUNG PLAYERS
GETTING STRONGER AS THEY LEARN

WE NEED SOMETHING TO LOOK FORWARD TO
SO SPORT HAS A PLACE FOR SURE
WE NEED TO HAVE THIS DISTRACTION
ENGLAND'S DONE WELL AND MORE

THERE'S A BUZZ IN THE AIR THAT'S EXCITING
HOPE IS WITH OUR TEAMS
ITS REMARKABLE AND SPECIAL
THERE'S HOPE FOR OUR SPORTS IT SEEMS

COME ON ENGLAND YOU CAN DO IT
IT LIFTS OUR SPIRITS FOR NOW
EVEN IF YOU DON'T LIKE SPORT
YOU ARE INTO IT ANYHOW

WE LOST THE FINAL ON PENALTIES
IT WAS SUCH A SHAME
ENGLAND HAS A BRILLIANT TEAM
NO ONE IS TO BLAME

THE 2020 OLYMPICS

2021

TOKYO IS HOSTING THE GAMES
WITH ALL THE COVID SCARE
WITHIN A STATE OF EMERGENCY
THE ATHLETES ARE NOW THERE

FANS WON'T BE THERE TO SUPPORT THEM
BUT THE ATHLETES HAVE TRAINED SO MUCH
SO THEY ALL GO ON REGARDLESS
THEY'RE LACKING THE HUMAN TOUCH

COVID HAS STOPPED SOME ATHLETES
IT'S A SHAME THAT THIS IS SO
IT DOESN'T SEEM THE SAME AT ALL
AND SOME OF THEM HAD TO GO

RESTRICTIONS ARE IN PLACE THERE
SO THE VIRUS DOESN'T SPREAD
I HOPE IT WORKS TO SOME EXTENT
IT FILLS MY HEART WITH DREAD

I REALLY HOPE THAT IT GOES OKAY
SO COMPETITORS REACH THEIR DREAMS
THAT ALL THE TRAINING WORKS FOR THEM
FOR EACH COUNTRY AND THEIR TEAMS

AS I WATCH THE GAMES I'M HOPEFUL
THAT ALL GOES ACCORDING TO PLAN
AND ALL THE EVENTS THAT TAKE PLACE
GO AHEAD AS WELL AS THEY CAN

FULLY VACCINATED 2021

I HAD MY FIRST JAB THAT WAS BRILLIANT
I FELT A BIT SAFER WOW
MY SECOND WAS TWELVE WEEKS AFTER
I'M FULLY VACCINATED NOW

I HOPE IT GIVES ME CONFIDENCE
TO DO NORMAL THINGS ONCE MORE
I HAVE BECOME A BIT OF A RECLUSE
THE PANDEMIC HAD LEFT ME RAW

THINGS HAVE MOVED ON SO QUICKLY
THE VACCINES ARE DOING THEIR THING
WE ARE ALL SO VERY LUCKY
TO GET BACK TO WHAT LIFE WILL BRING

THE SIDE EFFECTS I HAD A FEW
IT WAS WORTH IT FOR THE PROTECTION
SOON ALL ADULTS WILL HAVE HAD A JAB
THAT'S WHAT'S IN THE PROJECTION

IT'S STILL TOO EARLY TO DO TOO MUCH
WE'RE NOT FREE FROM COVID YET
WE MAY HAVE TO HAVE A BOOSTER SHOT
ALONG WITH OUR FLU JABS I BET

HOPEFULLY WE'RE ON THE RIGHT TRACK
IT DEPENDS ON US NOT TO FUSS
WE DON'T WANT ANY MORE LOCKDOWNS
ENJOY BUT PLEASE DON'T RUSH

ONCE THE VACCINES HAVE DONE THEIR JOB
THE WORLD WILL BE SAFE ONCE MORE
FINGERS CROSSED WE ARE BEATING IT
SO IT WON'T SHOW UP AT OUR DOOR

26
A NEW BEGINNING

SO NOW IT'S A NEW BEGINNING
A TIME TO REFLECT AND ADJUST
A NEW NORM IS EMERGING
A NEED FOR FAITH AND TRUST

WE KNOW THAT CHANGES ARE AFOOT
NOTHING WILL BE QUITE THE SAME
WE ALL MOVE ON REGARDLESS
BUT THE MEMORIES STILL REMAIN

NOTHING CAN TURN BACK TIME ITS TRUE
LIVES AND BUSINESSES HAVE BEEN LOST
SO MANY HAVE LOST THEIR LIVES WITH THIS
WE ARE STILL COUNTING THE COST

WE TENTIVELY VENTURE OUT AGAIN
THINGS ARE SO MUCH DIFFERENT NOW
KEEPING A SAFE DISTANCE APART
WE HAVE TO MOVE ON SOMEHOW

HIDING BEHIND OUR FACE MASKS
WE GO TO PLACES WE ONCE KNEW
THIS IS A NEW BEGINNING FOR US
REDISCOVERING THINGS TO DO

THERE'S A LIGHT AT THE END OF THE TUNNEL
AS THE SUN SHINES THROUGH THE RAIN
A NEW BEGINNING EMERGES
TO RETURN TO OUR LIVES ONCE AGAIN

WE HAVE A NEW BEGINNING
AND A BRAND NEW START
LETS GET THINGS BACK TO NORMAL
WE MUST DO THIS FROM THE HEART

IT WON'T BE QUITE THE SAME
BUT WE HAVE TO TAKE A CHANCE
A BRAND NEW BEGINNING
TO BRING BACK LOVE AND ROMANCE

PEOPLE WILL MEET UP AGAIN
HUGS AND CUDDLES WHEN WE MEET
GOING OUT AND MEETING PEOPLE
IS A NEW BEGINNING TREAT

SOON SOCIAL DISTANCING
WILL ALL BE IN THE PAST
CHILDREN WILL BE BACK IN SCHOOL
WE HOPE THAT IT WILL LAST

WE HAVE SO MUCH TO REPAIR
LOTS OF DAMAGE HAS BEEN DONE
THE NHS NEEDS HEALING NOW
AND A RESSESSION HAS BEGUN

THIS NEW BEGINNING HELPS US
TO REBUILD WHAT WAS BEFORE
NOTHING WILL BE QUITE THE SAME
SOME THINGS WILL BE NO MORE

GRIEVING FOR OUR LOVED ONES
LOST IN BATTLE ALONG THE WAY
LETS ALL PULL TOGETHER NOW
OUR NEW BEGINNING STARTS TODAY

27

REMEMBERING

NOW IS THE TIME TO REMEMBER
ALL THE PEOPLE WHO LOST THEIR LIVES
AS THE VIRUS GOES ON IN THE BACKGROUND
IT'S STILL WAITING AND STILL SURVIVES

WE MUST NOT TAKE THINGS FOR GRANTED
AS WE REMEMBER ALL THAT HAS BEEN
WE MOVE ON TOGETHER GRADUALLY
WITH A VIRUS THAT CANNOT BE SEEN

WE REMEMBER ALL THE FRONT LINE STAFF
WE CANNOT THANK THEM ENOUGH
WITHOUT THEM WE WOULD HAVE PERISHED
ALONG WITH THE OTHER BAD STUFF

SO AS WE MOVE ON TO NORMALLITY
REMEMBERING ALL THE SAD PAIN
NOTHING CAN STOP THE MEMORIES
WE MUST NEVER REPEAT THIS AGAIN

THROUGHOUT THE COVID CRISIS
SO MANY LIVES WERE LOST
WE MAY BE GETTING OUR LIVES BACK
BUT NOW WE ARE COUNTING THE COST

LESSONS MUST BE LEARNED FROM IT
WE MUST ALWAYS STAY SAFE FROM IT'S WRATH
COVID 19 WAS HORRENDOUS FOR ALL
AS WE REEL FROM THE AFTERMATH

VACCINE 2021

EVENTUALLY THE TIME HAD COME
TO RECEIVE MY FIRST VACCINE JAB
I WAS SO EXCITED BY THIS
THANK GOODNESS AND THANKS TO THE LAB

IT WAS A COVID LIFELINE FOR US
WE WERE OVER THE MOON WHEN IT CAME
WE WERE ALL STILL IN LOCKDOWN
THERE WE ARE STILL TO REMAIN

AS MORE PEOPLE RECEIVE THEIR JABS
THE BETTER OUR CHANCES WILL BE
I'M HALFWAY THERE TO ESCAPING NOW
IT CAN'T COME SOON ENOUGH FOR ME

MORE PEOPLE HAVE RECEIVED THEIR JABS
IT'S AMAZING HOW FAST ITS ROLLED OUT
PEOPLE WANT THIS TO BE OVER NOW
THEY WANT TO GET OUT AND ABOUT

SOON THE RESTRICTIONS ARE LIFTED
SCHOOLS ARE THE FIRST TO GO BACK
THE REST WILL FOLLOW SHORTLY
ITS TIME TO CUT US SOME SLACK

THE VACCINE I HAD WAS BRILLIANT
BUT IT CAME WITH SOME SIDE EFFECTS
SOME COUNTRIES HAD BANNED IT FOR SAFETY
UNTIL ITS PROVED SAFE NO REGRETS

THIS SLOWS DOWN THE ROLL OUT IMMENSELY
IT NEEDS SORTING OUT VERY FAST
I'VE HAD MY FIRST DOSE AND SOME SIDE
EFFECTS
I HOPE THAT THEY DO NOT LAST

THE VACCINE IS SO IMPORTANT
TO HELP US CONTROL THIS COVID
WE NEED TO GET THE VACCINE
SO WE CAN ALL GET RID

THE ONLY HOPE FOR US NOW
IS TO MAKE US ALL AWARE
THE VIRUS HAS KILLED MANY PEOPLE
BUT THE VACCINE CAN GET US THERE

WE WANT TO RETURN TO NORMALITY
IT'S GETTING OUT OF HAND
THE BEST THING NOW IS THE VACCINE
SO PEOPLE HAVE TO UNDERSTAND

WE KEEP OUR FINGERS AND TOES CROSSED
THAT EVERYTHING WORKS OUT OKAY
THIS IS THE BEST LINE OF DEFECE
TO MAKE COVID NINETEEN GO AWAY

29

TWENTY TWENTY ONE

I WANT MY OLD LIFE BACK
AS IT WAS BEFORE ALL THIS
I WANT TO FEEL AND TOUCH AGAIN
TO HUG AND STEEL A KISS

I WANT TO SEE FRIENDS AND FAMILY
ITS SO LONG SINCE THEY WERE HERE
I MISS THEM EACH AND EVERY DAY
THIS IS NOT A GOOD START TO THE YEAR

I WAS GLAD TO GET RID OF THE OLD YEAR
BUT THIS ONE IS JUST THE SAME
THE VIRUS IS MUTATING NOW
SO WE'RE IN A LOCKDOWN AGAIN

IN THE YEAR TWENTY TWENTY
WE HAD A YEAR FROM HELL
SO MUCH CHAOS AROUND ME
MY LIFE IS A MESS AS WELL

LOOKING FORWARD IN TWENTY TWENTY ONE
THERE'S SO MUCH I STILL HAVE TO DO
I WANT TO SEE A FUTURE AGAIN
I MUST GET IN THAT VACCINE QUEUE

I'VE NEVER BEEN SO EXCITED
I WAITED UNTIL I COULD GO
BRAVING THE FREEZING ICY COLD
I HAD MY JAB DESPITE THE SNOW

THIS IS LIKE THROWING A LIFELINE
IT GIVES US ALL SOME HOPE
TO HELP US GET OUT OF THIS LOCKDOWN
SO PEOPLE THEN MIGHT COPE

MY SECOND JAB IS DUE IN MAY
THE SPRING WILL SOON BE HERE
LETS HOPE THE VIRUS GOES AWAY
WE DON'T WANT TO LIVE IN FEAR

WHEN WILL ALL THIS MADNESS END?

AS I SIT AND REFLECT
I FEEL DISTRESSED
ANOTHER DAY HAS GONE
I AM SO DEPRESSED

WHEN WILL ALL THIS MADNESS END?
I FEAR IT WON'T GO AWAY
MONTHS HAVE FLOWN AND DISAPEARED
THE VIRUS IS HERE TO STAY

I FEEL SO FRUSTRATED
THERE'S SO MUCH THAT I WANT TO DO
NOTHING IS THE SAME ANYMORE
IT'S THE SAME FOR OTHERS TOO

I WAKE UP IN THE MORNINGS
THINKING ITS ALL BEEN A DREAM
MAYBE TODAY ITS ALL OVER
NOW THAT WE HAVE A VACCINE

I WANT TO GO OUT AND BE FREE AGAIN
LIKE GOING TO VISIT A FRIEND
I WANT THINGS TO BE NORMAL
OH WHEN WILL THIS MADNESS END

WHERE HAS ALL THE TIME GONE?

WHERE HAS ALL THE TIME GONE?
IT SEEMS TO HAVE GONE SO FAST
NOT BEING ABLE TO GO ANYWHERE
OUR VISIONS ARE ALL IN THE PAST

WHERE HAS ALL THE TIME GONE?
WE HAVE NO FUTURE YET
STILL IN LOCKDOWN NUMBER THREE
HOW MUCH WORSE CAN THIS GET?

WHERE HAS ALL THE TIME GONE?
WE NEED TO REGAIN OUR CONTROL
NOTHING CAN RESTART OUR LIVES JUST YET
WE NEED A FUTURE GOAL

WHERE HAS ALL THE TIME GONE?
WHAT LIES AHEAD WE DON'T KNOW
WE NEED A FUTURE NOT JUST A PAST
ONCE WE LET THE RESTRICTIONS GO

THINGS HAVE CHANGED

THINGS HAVE CHANGED IN THE WORLD WE
KNEW
NOTHING WILL BE THE SAME
EVERYTHING HAS BEEN RUINED BY US
AROUND US THERE'S HEARTACHE AND PAIN

HAVING SAID THAT WE MUST STAY STRONG
WE KNOW THAT LIFE IS STRANGE
POSITIVE THINKING GIVES US HOPE
WHEN THE VIRUS IS OUT OF RANGE

WE LIVE IN HOPE WE LOOK AHEAD
TWENTY, TWENTY ONE IT'S OKAY
VARIANT STRAINS ARE NOW RISING
WHICH MAY TAKE OUR FREEDOM AWAY

THIS HAS GONE ON FOR SO LONG NOW
WHERE HAS ALL THAT TIME GONE?
EVERYTHING STOPPED SO ABRUPTLY
WHAT THE HELL HAS JUST GONE ON?

ALL WE HAVE LEFT IT SEEMS TO ME
IS WHAT'S CALLED THE NEW NORM
NOT THE SAME AS IT ONCE WAS
NEW NORM HAS NOW BEEN BORN

LIFE GOES ON REGARDLESS
CHANGE IS ACCEPTED IT SEEMS
THINGS ARE NOT THE SAME ANYMORE
WE HAVE NEW HOPES AND DREAMS

VARIANTS

WE NOW HAVE A LOT OF VARIANTS
MUTATIONS OF THE VIRUS STRAIN
THIS IS QUITE UNNERVING
AS THE VIRUS STILL REMAINS

FOREIGN TRAVEL IS RESTRICTED
A TRAFFIC LIGHT SYSTEM IS IN PLACE
THE VACCINE MAY NOT WORK AS WELL
THAT TAKES THE SMILE OFF MY FACE

QUARANTINE IS SO IMPORTANT
TO TRY AND STOP THE SPREAD
THIS IS GOING ON RELENTLESSLY
SCARY THOUGHTS ARE IN MY HEAD

THE VACCINE MAY NEED TWEAKING
TO MAKE IT SAFE FOR EVERYONE
WE STRIVE TO BEAT THE VIRUS
WE WON'T GIVE UP UNTIL ITS GONE

ROADMAP TO RECOVERY

THERE'S A ROAD MAP TO RECOVERY
THAT APPEARS TO BE ON TRACK
SO HOPEFULLY THIS MEANS
WE'LL GET OUR OLD LIVES BACK

IT HAS TO BE DONE GRADUALLY
OR RESTRICTIONS WILL RETURN
WEAR MASKS AND KEEP SAFE DISTANCING
BUT SOME PEOPLE NEVER LEARN

THIS PANDEMIC ISN'T OVER YET
SO WE MUST STICK TO THE RULES
WE'RE GETTING MUCH MORE FREEDOM
THE CHILDREN ARE BACK IN SCHOOLS

WE MUSTN'T BE COMPLACENT
THIS IS FAR FROM OVER YET
VARIANTS ARE GETTINIG THROUGH
THERE WILL BE MANY MORE I BET

LETS HOPE AND PRAY ITS OVER
AS THE VACCINES DO THEIR BIT
TO GET OUR FREEDOM BACK AGAIN
LIKE IT WAS BEFORE IT HIT

I'M KEEPING MY FINGERS CROSSED
THAT THE VIRUS IS CONTAINED
I'M LOOKING FORWARD TO SEEING
ANY SHOPS THAT HAVE REMAINED

I'VE BEEN VERY FRIGHTENED
NOT DARING TO VENTURE OUT
I'VE GOT TO REGAIN MY CONFIDENCE
TO START TO GET OUT AND ABOUT

WE DON'T WANT ANY MORE LOCKDOWNS
WE'VE HAD MORE THAN ENOUGH
THE MISSING YEAR WAS HORRENDOUS
LIFE FOR EVERYONE WAS ROUGH

ALTHOUGH IT SEEMS RESTRICTIONS
ARE GETTING LESS AS THEY RELAX
WE MUST TAKE EACH STEP RESPONSIBLY
GET OUR JABS AND PROTECT TO THE MAX

PAST MISTAKES MUST BE HEEDED
SO WE CAN CONTINUE TO SURVIVE
WE MUST ALL BE THANKFUL NOW
ALL WE WANT IS TO STAY ALIVE

THE EASING OF RESTRICTIONS

July 2021

EVENTUALLY RESTRICTIONS WERE EASED
ALTHOUGH SOME THOUGHT IT TOO SOON
THE ELDERLY WERE CAUTIOUS
YOUNGSTERS WERE OVER THE MOON

CASES HAVE RISEN ABRUPTLY
THIS PANDEMIC ISN'T DONE
WE HAVE TO START BEING SENSIBLE
WITHOUT SPOILING EVERYONE'S FUN

I CAN SEE THIS ENDING UP IN TEARS
ITS ONLY A MATTER OF TIME
MASKS ARE NO LONGER COMPULSARY
BUT I WILL STILL WEAR MINE

I MUST ADMIT I FEEL FRIGHTENED
IS IT TOO MUCH TOO SOON
I DON'T WANT TO THINK NEGATEVELY
OR BURST ANYONE'S BALLOON

SOCIAL DISTANCING HAS BEEN REMOVED
SAFETY IS MOVING AWAY
I'M GOING TO BE VERY NERVOUS
THAT'S ALL I HAVE TO SAY

FOR THE MOMENT ANYTHING GOES
RESTRICTIONS HAVE ALL BEEN EASED
WHY DO I FEEL APPREHENSIVE?
WHEN I REALLY SHOULD BE PLEASED

I SUPPOSE THAT I'M BEING SCEPTICAL
TOO MUCH IS HAPPENING FAST
I'M FRIGHTENED IT WILL GET BAD AGAIN
AND OUR FREEDOM WILL NOT LAST

I HOPE MY FEARS ARE UNFOUNDED
AND THAT IT WILL BE OKAY
THE LAST THING THAT WE WANT IS THAT
OUR FREEDOM IS TAKEN AWAY

36

THE OPENING OF ALL RESTRICTIONS

THE RESTRICTIONS ARE ALL GOING
WE'LL BE BACK TO NORMAL SOON
EVERYONE IS EXCITED BY THIS
THEY ARE ALL OVER THE MOON

NOT LONG NOW BEFORE IT'S DUE
SOON WE CAN ALL RELAX
BACK TO DOING THE THINGS WE LIKE
WE WILL BE BACK ON THE TRACKS

LOOKING FORWARD TO FREEDOM
TO RETURN TO SOME NORMALITY
TO THE POINT WHERE WE LEFT OFF
MOVING ON TO A NEW REALITY

BECAUSE OF THE INDIAN VARIANT
RESTRICTIONS ARE STILL IN PLACE
ALTHOUGH WE'RE DISAPPOINTED
WE NEED THIS JUST IN CASE

NOW WE'LL HAVE TO WAIT A WHILE
TO SEE HOW THINGS PAN OUT
HOPEFULLY WE WON'T WAIT LONG
WE DON'T WANT THIS VIRUS ABOUT

VACCINATIONS ARE BEING ROLLED OUT AGAIN
SO THE YOUNG ONES GET THEIRS DONE
IF IT WORKS OUT OKAY WE MIGHT JUST GET
OUR LIVES BACK AND HAVE SOME FUN

SLOWLY WE ARE GETTING THERE
ITS BEEN A LONG JOURNEY ITS TRUE
BUT IT WILL BE WORTH WAITING FOR
WHEN WE BEGIN OUR LIVES ANEW

37

HISTORY

WE'RE ALL PART OF HISTORY NOW
WHEN THE WHOLE WORLD WENT MAD
WE DIDN'T REALISE AT THE TIME
THE GOOD THINGS WE ONCE HAD

THE NORMALITY OF LIFE BEFORE
GRADUALLY FADED AWAY
WE HAD TO LIVE WITH COVID
BECAUSE IT'S HERE TO STAY

NOTHING CAN CONSOLE US
ITS BEEN SO HARD TO ENDURE
ALL THAT WE CAN HOPE FOR NOW
IS A VACCINE OR A CURE

THIS IS HISTORY IN THE MAKING
WE HAVE MANY TALES TO TELL
ABOUT OUR TIME WITH COVID
DURING THIS LIVING HELL

WE'VE ALL GOT TO LIVE WITH THIS
FOREVER AND A DAY
BECAUSE THIS DREADFUL VIRUS
WILL NEVER GO AWAY

WE WILL TELL OUR CHILDREN
WHO WILL TELL THEIR CHILDREN TOO
THIS WILL ALL BE HISTORY
WE MANAGED TO SEE IT THROUGH

FUTURE GENERATIONS MUST LEARN
NEVER TO LET YOUR GUARD DOWN
NATURE DOESN'T TAKE PRISONERS
IT WILL ALWAYS WEAR THE CROWN

WE MUST TAKE CARE OF OUR PLANET
WE NEED TO PRESERVE WHAT WE'VE GOT
THINGS WILL ONLY GET WORSE FOR US
NOW OUR WORLD IS GETTING TOO HOT

38

I MET UP WITH MY GRANDKIDS

SUCH A SPECIAL OCCASION
FILLED MY HEART WITH JOY
I LOVED TO SEE THE GRANDKIDS
I GOT THE LITTLE ONE'S A TOY

I MET UP WITH MY GRANDKIDS
WE CAUGHT UP WITH LOST TIME
MY GREAT GRANDKIDS HAD GROWN
I'M SO PROUD THAT THEY ARE MINE

IT FELT SO NORMAL AGAIN
MY HEART FILLED WITH PRIDE
I WAS SO EMOTIONAL
WITH TEARS OF JOY I CRIED

I MET UP WITH MY GRANDKIDS
A MILESTONE IN MY HEART
THE DARKEST ERA HAD ENDED
A NEW BEGINNING WILL NOW START

I MET UP WITH MY GRANDKIDS
IT HAD BEEN SUCH A LONG TIME
I LOVED EVERY MINUTE WITH THEM
I LOVE THESE GRANDKIDS OF MINE

WHEN I FINALLY MET THEM
IT LIFTED MY SPIRIT SO MUCH
MY DEPRESSION SIMPLY FADED AWAY
I GOT HUGS AND WE COULD TOUCH

I'VE GOT NINE LOVELY GRANDKIDS
AND FIVE GREAT GRANDKIDS TOO
I GOT TO SEE THEM ALL AGAIN
JUST LIKE WE USED TO DO

I MET UP WITH MY GRANDKIDS
IT WAS SUCH A LOVELY DAY
CREATING PRECIOUS MEMORIES
NOTHING CAN TAKE THEM AWAY

THERE WILL ALWAYS BE A FUTURE

THERE WILL ALWAYS BE A FUTURE
LIFE GOES ON AS NATURE DOES
OUR LIFESPAN IS SHORT LIVED
THE FUTURE ALL STEMS FROM US

WE CAN START TO SOLVE OUR PROBLEMS
EVEN THOUGH THERE ARE SO MANY
BE KIND TO ONE AND OTHER NOW
KIND HEARTS DON'T COST A PENNY

AS WE REGAIN OUR FREEDOM
LIFE GOES FORWARD ONCE AGAIN
FOR THOSE WHO LOST THEIR LIVES
IN OUR THOUGHTS THEY WILL REMAIN

THERE WILL ALWAYS BE A FUTURE
OUR GENERATIONS HAVE MOVED ON
WE'LL LOOK BACK AT OUR FUTURE
LONG AFTER THE VIRUS HAS GONE

WE MUST CLEAN UP OUR PLANET
ERADICATE ALL THE GERMS
LIVE OUR LIVES AS BEST WE CAN
LIVING ON NATURES TERMS

ITS UP TO OUR GENERATION
TO MAKE THE CHANGES NOW
THERE WILL ALWAYS BE A FUTURE
OUR WORLD WILL SURVIVE SOMEHOW

YEARS FROM NOW

AS I SIT HERE AND WRITE IN MY JOURNAL
I STILL CAN'T BELIEVE THAT ITS TRUE
SO MUCH HAS HAPPENED IT'S SO SURREAL
THERE WAS NOTHING THAT WE COULD DO

HOWEVER HARD WE TRIED OUR BEST
NOTHING SEEMED TO DO ANY GOOD
WE ADAPTED OUR LIVES TO COPE WITH IT
WE DID EVERYTHING THAT WE COULD

I REFUSE TO WRITE MORE NEGATIVE WORDS
NOW IS THE TIME TO MOVE ON
WE'RE ALL SAILING IN THE SAME BOAT
WE WANT THIS VIRUS TO BE GONE

I'VE NO IDEA HOW THINGS WILL WORK OUT
BUT HERE'S WHERE MY JOURNAL ENDS
I WANT TO SEE MY FAMILY AGAIN
AND MEET UP AGAIN WITH MY FRIENDS

I END THIS WITH MUCH LOVE AND HOPE
BIG HUGS TO YOU ONE AND ALL
SOCIAL CONTACT IS LONG OVERDUE
WE'LL MEET IN PERSON NOT A CALL

LETS ENJOY OUR NEW FOUND FREEDOM
THIS MIGHT BE AS GOOD AS IT GETS
LETS HOPE LIFE GETS BACK TO NORMAL
WITHOUT HAVING TOO MANY REGRETS

NONE OF KNOW WHAT THE FUTURE HOLDS
WE CAN ONLY HOPE FOR THE BEST
BE KIND TO EACH OTHER EVERYDAY
OUR WORLD HAS BEEN PUT THROUGH A TEST

41

GUEST AUTHOR
JACK NEWMAN

A big thankyou to Jack Newman who has kindly donated one of his poems to be included in this book. Jack has been co-author in a number of books we wrote together.
Including Oceans Apart and Tandem Tales.
Jack lives in Australia with his family.

Jack Newman

TELL US A STORY GRANDAD

IN THE OLDEN DAYS BEFORE THIS VIRUS HAD
ITS WAY

THERE WERE NO SUCH THINGS AS LOCKDOWNS
AND PEOPLE COULD TRAVEL FREELY TO ANY
TOWN
IT DIDN'T MATTER IF IT WAS INTERSTATE
OR OVERSEES TO VISIT FAMILY OR MATES

KIDS COULD GO TO SCHOOL EACH DAY
AND GATHER IN THEIR GROUNDS TO PLAY
STADIUMS WERE PACKED WITH PEOPLE SON
EACH WEEKEND CHEERING THEIR TEAMS ON

THERE WERE TOILET ROLLS APLENTY IN THE
ISLES
AND PAPER MONEY WAS ACCEPTED WITH A
SMILE
NO NEED TO WEAR FANCY MASKS THEN
AND STAND WELL AWAY FROM OLD FRIENDS

IT WAS A TIME TO BE CAREFREE AND STAY
CALM
NOT HAVE CHEMICALS INJECTED IN YOUR ARI
OR HAVE A NURSE TEST YOU FOR VIRUS WOE
EVERY TIME YOU HAD A COUGH OR RUNNY
NOSE

NO SON THAT WAS A TIME LONG AGO WHEN
WE DIDN'T REALISE HOW GOOD WE HAD IT
THEN
AND HOW FREE WE WERE TO KISS AND HUG
UNTIL WE LOST IT ALL TO A TINY BUG

THE AUTHOR

Pamela Griffiths nee Cocker was born in Sheffield in September 1952; Widow of Clive Griffiths. She has three children, a stepson, nine grandchildren and 5 great grandchildren Pamela has a diploma in freelance journalism, a diploma in quality management and is retired from working for the NHS as a Quality and Development Manager. She lives in Loxley, Sheffield with her partner Andy Hoffman.

Pamela won a National Local Poetry competition in 2011 with 'Home Sweet Home in Loxley Valley'. She has also won the National Poetry competition 'Great Britain' with her poem 'The Best of British'.in 2016. Her work has been published in over eighty poetry anthologies. Pamela's own poetry books include 'Expressions of Life', 'Moments in Time', 'Life is a Spiral Staircase', A Sheffield Lass' and Under a Blood Red Moon', Fur Babies, Bossy the bunny series of 10 children's books.

Control the Demon' was the first novel she had published in 1991 by Minerva Press. 'The Stamp Master' was the first novel in the DCI Chrissie Charles detective thrillers along with 'Heartless' and 'The Impaler The trilogy has received some five star reviews. Pamela is currently working on another children's book 'Kimba the kitten'.
Over the years Pamela has donated and contributed many of her books for various charities and fund raising events.

For more information please visit:

Website - www.pamelagriffiths.com

Twitter - @pamg56

Author fan page on Facebook - Author Pamela Griffiths